Imprint

Editor and publisher: Verlag Anton Plenk
Koch-Sternfeld-Straße 5 – D-83471 Berchtesgaden
Fon: 00 49-86 52-44 74
Fax: 00 49-86 52-6 62 77
E-Mail: Plenk-Verlag@t-online.de
http://www.Plenk-Verlag.com

Pictures: Werner Mittermeier

Text: Albert Hirschbichler

Editing: Stefanie Zweckl, Bischofswiesen

Setting and layout: GL-Werbestudio, Grassl&Lage, Berchtesgaden

Lithography: GL-Werbestudio, Grassl&Lage, Berchtesgaden

Translation: Barbara Hirschbichler, Schönau

Printing, overall production: Druckerei A. Plenk KG, Berchtesgaden

Printed on Galaxi Brilliant, 170 g/qm. Exclusive by Papier Union.

1st edition – summer 2010

Bibliographical information of the German Library:
The German Library lists this publication in the German National Bibliography
Detailed bibliographical data can be found on http://dnb.ddb.de
ISBN 978-3-940141-43-9

Werner Mittermeier · Albert Hirschbichler

Chiemgau
and
Berchtesgadener Land

VERLAG PLENK
BERCHTESGADEN

Table of contents

An enchanting holiday region

Many writers have celebrated this charming region in word and song. Scores of painters have depicted it in every colour and atmosphere, in oil and in watercolour. Its centre is Lake Chiemsee, which is also called "Bavarian Sea" due to its large white-blue surface. It is close to the Alps and embedded in undulating hills; its shores benefit from a relatively mild climate. Around Lake Chiemsee, spring starts two weeks earlier than in the Tegernsee Valley, for instance. When the yellow of the forsythia is reflected in the lake and contrasts with the white of the snow-covered mountains, an unforgettable magic lies in the air. Heralds of spring like snowdrop, daffodil and crocus turn the soft green meadows into colourful carpets. The merry wedding song of the blackbird and the other songbirds that have returned from their winter quarters sounds like a flute concert and delights our ear. The gentle sounds and sweet odours that spring brings with it dissipate all gloomy thoughts that have accumulated during the dark season.

Spring and summer blend into each other imperceptibly. Magnolias, cherry blossom and apple blossom follow close upon one another. If you don't hurry you will miss the dark blue blossoms of the acaulescent gentian on the alpine pastures. There is so much to see and to discover, and you want to be everywhere at the same time – at the water, on the moors and in the mountains. The snow retreats to the heights so that the space is cleared for the gentle blossoms which wondrously start to burgeon. When the snow melts metre by metre and the ground becomes saturated with water, the small roots, bulbs and tubers bringing forth the most magnificent blossoms are activated. Like gossamer are the violet little bells of soldanella alpina (alpine snowbell) with their thin red stems. They stand the frost which in April and May might easily occur at an altitude of around 1000 metres. Then the big, bright blossoms of winter roses look at us, too, and the delicate blossoms of the crocuses sprout through the cold ground.

When the leaves of beech and oak trees have fully unfolded and the mighty sycamore maple shines in bright green, the farmers set about driving their cattle up to the alpine pastures. However, this cattle drive has changed fundamentally since the old days – modern technology can't be averted. For our ancestors the cattle drive was a time-consuming and labour-intensive matter, but also an important annual event. For the alpine herdsmen and dairymaids, summer on the alpine pastures was presumably a pleasant time in spite of the hard work, the dangers, the worries and the responsibility for the cattle. They were occupied with milking the cows and dairy processing. In former times, cheese was made at every alp. Today it is almost exclusively young cattle that are driven up to alpine pastures since they don't have to be milked. Moreover, driving the animals up on foot is for the most part a thing of the past.

Anyway, the hiker strolling from one alp to another takes pleasure in the sound of the cow bells. What he will largely miss, though, is the pretty dairymaids or else some alpine herdsmen from whom he would gladly accept the offer of a glass of fresh milk.

Not infrequently the huts are closed and there is not a living soul anywhere near. Staff is expensive nowadays. Instead, the farmer or his wife use

Right:
On Lake Chiemsee,
near Breitbrunn

their off-road vehicle to drive up to the alp once every day to check if everything is all right. During the rest of the time the animals are left to themselves.

Hiking is a popular activity among the tourists in the Chiemgau. On sunny, hot days many a tourist may not be inclined to toil up a mountain. People who come from the plains should take note, though, that on the mountains it is not unbearably hot. In normal summer weather the temperature decreases by 1° Centigrade per 100 altimeters. For example, if the midday temperature in Grassau is 30°, we can reckon with 18° on the summit of Mount Hochgern (1748 m). For this reason a jacket or pullover must be part of the standard equipment in our rucksack even in summer.

The wooden shingles on the roofs of alps have been weighted down with stones

Right:
Fog in the valley of the River Tiroler Ache

The mountains are beautiful in any season, no matter whether they are covered with glistening snow, which enables us to race downhill on fast skis, or whether they delight us with the splendour of the colourful flowers. One thing is certain: the high season for hikers and climbers starts in September. Autumn is the great time for enjoying the sun on the heights.

In late autumn, the law that the temperature decreases with increasing altitude is not always true. It can frequently be observed that the air on the mountains is several degrees warmer than the air in the valleys. It is then that Lake Chiemsee is hidden by its famous fog. The whole lake lies under a thick blanket of fog which is not more

Right:
Summit of Mount
Kampenwand
(1668 m)

Double page (overleaf):
In the valley of the
River Tiroler Ache

A mountain farm

than fifty, one hundred or two hundred metres thick. But this unpleasant, clammy fog is no insurmountable problem in the Chiemgau. By car you will quickly get to the foot of a mountain: Hochgern, Hochplatte or Geigelstein, Hörndlwand or Sonntagshorn. Mostly it only takes a few determined strides, and we step out into the warm sun. Furthermore the Chiemgau boasts a number of fine summits that can be reached by cable car. The best known of these are doubtlessly Mount Kampenwand and Mount Hochfelln. The valley station of the Kampenwand cable car is at Hohenaschau, that of Hochfelln cable car at Bergen. Another mountain that has to be mentioned in this connection is Hochries which lies in the west, in the direction of the valley of the River Inn. You have to go to Grainbach by car or public

service vehicle and board the cable car there. Thus it only takes minutes to get out of the cold fog into the blazing sun.

It is the clear view in this season that makes autumn the favourite time for hikes in the mountains. At the northern rim of the Alps there is another phenomenon that greatly matters to us mountaineers: foehn. This is a falling wind that comes from the south and crosses the Alpine divide, bringing the northern rim of the Alps wonderful weather and clear air. In foehn conditions visibility is tremendous. You can perceive Mount Zugspitze in the west and Mount Dachstein in the east with your naked eye. The reason for designating October the most beautiful month in the mountains is the blaze of colours of the forests up to the tree line. The yellow and copper crowns of sycamore maples and beeches are ablaze with light. The bright colours of nature are intensified by the first snow on the summits. If you ever see such glorious days, you will never forget them. In my own heart they also evoke a feeling of gratitude.

13

On the Deutsche Alpenstraße

Deutsche Alpenstraße

Germany's oldest scenic road

The so-called Deutsche Alpenstraße connects Lindau on Lake Constance with Berchtesgaden in the extreme south-east of the Free State of Bavaria. No fewer than 21 picturesque lakes, 25 castles and palaces as well as 64 spas lie along the route.

The development of this project is generally connected with the National Socialists, but this is not exactly right. It is true, the construction plan received strong impulse during the time of the Third Reich, but the origin of the idea and the beginning of its realization go back to the time after the First World War. At first the planners thought of an alpine hiking trail between Lake Constance and Lake Königssee, but with the emergence of motor traffic a road seemed more reasonable. Due to a lack of money, the planners only connected some already existing roads, in the confidence that someday the dream road through the German Alps would emerge. The Second World War brought problems of a different kind so that the project was not followed for a long time, nor was an extension of the road a priority during the economic boom of the post-war years. Later, environmental protection became important so that the Deutsche Alpenstraße is still patchwork, as it were. It leads along the northern rim of the Alps partly on A-roads and country roads, but there are some gaps which have to be bridged on devious routes. Not all parts of the route have been upgraded, and there are no consistent road numbers, but nobody is greatly disturbed by that.

However, it is a discomforting idea that the Alpenstraße might be a continuous band between Lindau and Berchtesgaden, generously enlarged or even multi-lane, which might attract huge numbers of car drivers from all over the world. Actually, the fragmentary state of the Alpenstraße does not need to be changed. Nobody will want to drive the 460-km-long route without stopping. It is presumably more rewarding to cherry-pick the most beautiful sections for short trips, or else divide the whole route into manageable stages. Not infrequently there are cultural sights along the road, and some side roads are certainly worth taking even if a toll might be due.

Königsbach, a mountain stream running into Lake Königssee

Double page (overleaf): Ramsau near Berchtesgaden – one of the most beautiful sections of the Deutsche Alpenstraße

Snowdrops

Course of the Deutsche Alpenstraße

The road starts quite inconspicuously in the town of Rothkreuz near Lindau and ends equally inconspicuously just after Marktschellenberg, at Hangendenstein, in the Berchtesgadener Land, right at the border to Austria. It does not really reach record heights when it crosses Oberjoch/Allgäu (1180 m) and Sudelfeld (1097 m), but these two mountain passes are high enough to offer nice views of the environs and the surrounding mountains, even of the 3000-metre-peaks of the Central Alps. Altogether, the most beautiful and impressive sections are the road to Oberstaufen via the so-called "Paradies" (paradise), the roads around Hindelang and Oberjoch, the sector between Garmisch-Partenkirchen and Lake Tegernsee (especially the route Wallgau – Vorderriss), and last but not least the upgraded road through the nature reserve of the Chiemgau Alps after Reit im Winkl. One third of the Deutsche Alpenstraße leads through the Bavarian part of Swabia. Near Füssen, which lies in the valley of the River Lech, it crosses the border to Upper Bavaria. The surroundings of Füssen abound with lakes. East of the town are the Ammergau Alps which with an area of 276 km² are Bavaria's largest nature reserve. There is no passage for cars through the mountain range, but there are two routes which lead around it: the northern route from Füssen via Steingaden, Eschelsbacher Brükke, Saulgrub, and Oberammergau to Linderhof (60 km), or the southern route via Reutte, Plansee, and Ammersattel to Linderhof (40 km), the latter leading through Austrian territory. The shorter alternative is the more interesting one as

Lake Simssee with Mount Wendelstein and Mount Breitenstein. Lake Simssee is one of the numerous lakes in the area of Rosenheim

Each season has its charm. Nature has inexhaustible treasures to offer. Every day is a present from God for which we express our deeply-felt gratitude

far as scenery is concerned, but if you decide for it you will miss cultural sights such as Steingaden, Wieskirche or Rottenbuch, which are all well worth seeing. The royal castle of Linderhof is the point where the eastern section of the Alpen-straße starts.

The road leads in an eastern direction through the Graswang Valley until, three kilometres south-east of Oberammergau, it joins the B 23, a through road. Then it passes Ettal Monastery, crosses Ettaler Sattel and, offering many nice views, winds down into the valley of the River Loisach. Garmisch-Partenkirchen, one of Bava-ria's most outstanding tourist centres, lies some kilometres to the south. From there, you can con-veniently reach the summit of Mount Zugspitze, Germany's highest mountain, by cog railway. The route leads eastwards through the Kankertal, the valley which forms the northern-most border of the mountains of the Wetterstein range. Near the village of Klais you reach the trough-like valley of the upper River Isar. If you want to – and in fact, you really should - make the side trip to Mitten-wald, the town of violin makers and painters, it is advisable to take the small winding road starting in Klais.

On the E 533, a well-extended road, you reach Wallgau via Krün. There the Alpenstraße is inter-rupted once more. Instead of taking the long way via Kochel and Bad Tölz you should continue on the narrow scenic toll road leading along the gravel-filled bed of the River Isar. After some 15 kilometres, at Vorderriß (here a side trip to the Eng valley and the so-called "Großer Ahornbo-den" is strongly recommended), you reach the next section of the Alpenstraße. Crossing Achen-pass (940 m), a not very striking mountain pass, you get into the Weißach valley with its green pastures. Famous places like Wildbad Kreuth and Kreuth are passed on the way to Rottach-Egern on Lake Tegernsee. In contrast to these places, which cater to wealthy tourists and spa guests, Schliersee, Fischbachau and Bayrischzell are rather quiet. When you are at Bayrischzell, you should not miss taking the cable car up Mount Wendelstein (1838m), the "Bavarian Rigi". Conti-nuing on the so-called "Sudelfeld" road, you will get fantastic views; however, the road ends at "Tatzelwurm".

There are two options: the northern road, a toll road, leads to Brannenburg, where you have access to the A 93 (Inntal motorway) which joins the A 8 (motorway between Munich and Salz-burg), which in turn takes you to Bernau on Lake Chiemsee. The southern road, more worthwhile and toll-free, leads to Oberaudorf, then for a short distance through Austrian territory, crossing the border again near Sachrang. From there the road runs through the Prien valley and finally takes you, via Aschau, to Bernau. At the rim of the expansive lowland of Lake Chiemsee, the Alpen-straße continues to Grassau, Marquartstein and Unterwössen, running along the River Tiroler Ache. After some kilometres of ascending road

Right:
Lake Chiemsee is also called the "Bavarian Sea". It lies in beautiful surroundings directly at the rim of the Alps.

you get to the renowned holiday resort of Reit im Winkl.

The following section of the Alpenstraße runs through the nature reserve of the Chiemgau Alps with its pristine lakes (Weitsee, Mittersee, Lödensee and Forchensee) and forests. This is certainly one of the most delightful parts of the whole Alpenstraße. Ruhpolding and Inzell are bypassed. Another highlight of the road is the gorge of the Weißbachschlucht. The winding road was blasted into the rock high above the bottom of the gorge, and the traveller gets a view of primordial landscapes. Near Schneizlreuth the road enters the valley of the River Saalach and follows it in the direction of Bad Reichenhall for a short distance. Shortly before reaching this town, famous for its salt and its spa facilities, you have to turn right in the direction of Schwarzbachwacht. The ascent to the top of the mountain pass (870 m) is the last before reaching the basin of Berchtesgaden. When you get to the top of the Schwarzbachwacht pass, the view is obstructed by trees, as if the Berchtesgaden mountains wanted to create suspense. After a few hundred metres, however, the road leaves the forest and, quite unexpectedly, a magnificent high mountain panorama presents itself before your eyes: the rugged Hochkalter range with the northern-most glacier of the Alps, the so-called Blaueis (blue ice), is directly in front of you. To the left you can see Watzmann with its massive western flank. The road leads down to the valley of Ramsau through green pastures. In these surroundings, it would almost be an offence to this corner of the earth if you only took the nearest way to the end of the Alpenstraße. The most beautiful side-trips take you to Lake Hintersee, Lake Königssee, Maria Gern at the foot of Mount Untersberg, and the Rossfeld mountain ring road.

Chiemgau – Chiemgau Alps

The expansive landscape around Lake Chiemsee, bordered by the River Inn in the west, the River Traun in the east, the mountains in the south and a not exactly determinable line running through the towns of Wasserburg and Trostberg, has been known as Chiemgau since the 8th century. Even before that time the Celts had settled in the area and the Romans had built a road. The name goes back to a settler called "Chiemmi", mentioned in a document dating from 744 AD, whose dwellings were situated where Chieming is today. First that part of the lake, then the whole lake and eventually the region were named after him. One part of the Chiemgau belongs to the administrative district of Rosenheim, another to that of Traunstein. Lake Chiemsee, the "Bavarian Sea", is its centre.

With an area of 80 square kilometres and a depth of up to 73 metres, Lake Chiemsee (which lies at an altitude of 518 m) is the biggest lake in Bavaria. It would even be bigger if the lake level had not been lowered by the deepening of the River Alz, which runs out of the lake, near Seebruck in the 19th century. On old maps, places like Grabenstätt and Winkl still lie directly on the lake shore. The lake owes its existence to the large Chiemsee Glacier, which melted towards the end of the last Ice Age, about 15.000 years ago. Apart from the Chiemsee basin, the glaciers of the Ice Age formed a number of hollows – today charming lakes, for instance Waginger See, Simssee, the lakes of Eggstätt-Hemhof and Seeon as well as many a mountain lake.

Landscape near Bernau with Lake Chiemsee in the background

The ice was up to 500 metres thick and transported huge amounts of debris. Where the ice melted, masses of gravel remained. These moraines today are visible as lines of hills which characterize the landscape. They are distinctly to be recognized around Bernau and Frasdorf, for example.

Around Lake Chiemsee, 18 full-time fishermen earn their living.

There is hardly any industry, but instead there is a beautiful landscape which is often used for farming. Once again it was the landscape painters who in the 19th century made the area widely known through their paintings. Since then the Chiemgau has been a traditional tourist region. The landscape is characterized by a lot of bodies of water, both rivers and lakes, by hill moors featuring a remarkable fauna, and by a view of the mountains, which are quite near, but not really high (none of them reaches the 2000-metre-mark). The most striking mountain is Mount Kampenwand (1668 m). Traditions and customs are held high in the area. In the villages you find rustic-style inns and beer gardens. It is a peculiarity of the Chiemgau that two cultural highlights are to be found in the middle of the water. On the island of Herrenchiemsee, King Ludwig II of Bavaria had his dreamlike castle built, and on the neighbouring island of Frauenchiemsee is the landmark of Lake Chiemsee, Frauenwörth Monastery.

Double page (overleaf):
Lake Chiemsee with the
island of Fraueninsel

May pole in Übersee
on Lake Chiemsee

Herrenchiemsee

In 1873, when Ludwig II of Bavaria acquired the incomparably lovely Herrenwörth, the present Herrenchiemsee, the island had already experienced a history of more than 2000 years. From the 13th century to the time of Secularisation, the island was the centre of a diocese, of which the "Altes Schloss" (old palace) and the "Inseldom" (island cathedral) still bear witness. A kind of quixotic melancholy and rather seclusive tendencies had prompted Ludwig to buy the island in Lake Chiemsee. Here his "new Versailles" was eventually to be created. During two journeys to Paris the king had studied all the details of Versailles Castle. In the palace of the Sun King, Louis XIV, he saw the consummate realization of royal glory which he wanted to emulate in a building of his own. When – forestalling some wood speculators – he could buy the island, the opportunity to fulfil his long-cherished plans offered itself at last.

Georg Dollmann was commissioned with the design of the "New Castle of Herrenchiemsee". After many alterations and extensions the foundation stone was laid on May 21, 1878. In spite of the great difficulties which the laying of the foundations and the transport of the building material across the lake posed, the builders, permanently urged on by the king, were able to complete the structural work of the tremendous construction as early as 1881.

The interior fittings are characterized by sumptuous splendour, with which Ludwig sought to surpass the French prototype. He had the most precious building materials brought from all over Europe.

Right:
The castle on the island of Herreninsel in Lake Chiemsee – built by the Bavarian "fairy-tale king" Ludwig II

Fitting the stairway, the state room and the king's living room with inlaid flooring, carved wainscoting and stucco marble panelling, with wall paintings and ceiling frescos, sculptures and valuable furniture took more than four years. The royal bedspread for the bedroom alone occupied twenty seamstresses for seven years.

The large mirror gallery became the main room of the castle. It is 98 metres long and extends over the whole garden front of the building. The dominating elements of the room with its ceiling-high windows on one side and the wall mirrors on the other are the 44 flambeaux and 33 large glass chandeliers. One wonders what it might have looked like when the room was lit at night by 2000 candles!

The king originally planned to get to his castle in a swan-shaped gondola hanging on a wire rope 50 metres above the lake – illuminated by Bengal light, of course – but in spite of the greatest endeavours of the engineers, this was not to be realized in the end. Altogether, Herrenchiemsee was the most ambitious and expensive of Ludwig's ventures. After a construction time of seven years (1878-1885), during which he exchanged Dollmann, the tardy architect, by Julius Hoffmann and spent 16 million gold mark, the cabinet exchequer reported bankruptcy. The death of Ludwig II in 1886 eventually signified the end of the project. The king had spent a total of nine days in the castle...

The inner courtyard of the former monastery on Herreninsel

The magnificent castle gardens on Herren-chiemsee are decorated with numerous fountains and sculptures

*Herrenchiemsee
Castle is modelled on
Versailles Castle in
France.*

View of the octagonal tower dating from the 11ᵗʰ century, the landmark of Fraueninsel; seen from the Carolingian gate hall

Right:
The convent buildings on Fraueninsel

Frauenchiemsee

Between Herrenchiemsee and Frauenchiemsee lies an uninhabited island called Krautinsel (cabbage island). There is only a vegetable garden for the convent on Frauenwörth, as Frauenchiemsee is also called. Compared to Herreninsel with its area of 3.28 km², Fraueninsel (0.15 km²) is a tiny island.

In the second half of the 8ᵗʰ century, Duke Tassilo III (746-788), the last of the Agilofings, founded a nunnery here. The old convent, an imperial diocese since the times of the Carolingians, existed until Secularisation in 1803, but was then abolished and finally founded once again by King Ludwig I of Bavaria. The Benedictine convent Frauenchiemsee is among the most ancient in Bavaria. Frauenwörth Minster, the church of the convent built around the turn of the millennium, is especially worth seeing.

The construction of the detached tower dates from the 10ᵗʰ century. In later years it was made higher, and in 1572 it received its characteristic onion dome, which has become the landmark of the island. The altars of the church, among them the high altar dating from 1694, were created in the Baroque period. In 1954 the convent church became famous among experts when Romanesque wall paintings were discovered. They were uncovered and conserved from 1961 to 1965. They date from around 1130 and rank among the most exquisite works of Romanesque fresco art showing Byzantine influence found in the Salzburg area.

About 300 people live on the little island, which can easily be surrounded on foot in half an hour.

Next to the convent there is a little village which in summer comes up with flower-bedecked houses

between old linden trees. Winding footpaths connect the houses with each other. Not infrequently, pottery is offered in or in front of the houses. The inn with its beer garden is a special attraction. The nuns displayed an amazing flexibility when they stopped running the tradition-rich school, boarding school and kindergarten in 1995. Without further ado they converted the rooms of the boarding school rooms into guest rooms and the classrooms into seminar rooms, and today they organize, among other events, manager seminars, congresses or party conventions.

Top:
The paddle steamer "Ludwig Fessler", built in 1926

Below:
The Carolingian gate hall dating from the 9th century

Sailing boats in front of Fraueninsel

Right:
Fraueninsel with Mount Hochgern

Right:
Kailbach with Mount
Kampenwand

Blue bell flower

Around the lake

The two, or rather three (including Krautinsel) islands, lie in the western part of the lake. It is called "Inselsee" (island lake), whereas the eastern part, which has a larger area, is called "Weitsee" (broad lake). A number of charming villages and small towns surround the lake. Starting with the first settlement, Chieming, on the eastern shore of the lake, and continuing in a clockwise direction, there are the following parishes: Grabenstätt, Übersee, Bernau, Prien, Rimsting, Gstadt, Breitbrunn, Lambach and Seebruck. A 60-kilometre-long road exlusively for bikers and hikers runs around the whole lake. While the southern shore consists of flat alluvial land – debris deposited by the River Tiroler Ache – the shore in the north-west, between Gstadt and Lambach, is a bluff. Between Rimsting and Breitbrunn there are hills consisting of the deposits left by the former Chiemsee Glacier, and when the basin filled with water these hills became peninsulas.

The diversity of landforms makes the shore area between the mouth of the River Prien and the town of Seebruck the most varied section of the whole lakeside. You can best make sure of this by using a bike. Since the construction of the Chiemsee cycleway, surrounding the lake on a bike has become very popular, and on weekend days in summer there are almost too many cyclists. For walks, too, the above-mentioned section – which can be dissected at will, of course – is the best option. There are no significant ascents, and one walks along either directly on the shore or else behind the zone of reeds, which offers protection to many birds and aquatic animals. If you are

Right:
Bathing beach near Gstadt, with a view of the island of Fraueninsel; in the background Mount Hochfelln and Mount Hochgern

lucky, you will be able to watch rare waterfowl, apart from swans and ducks.

Along the way there are quiet bays as well as some dispersed settlements and colourful marinas, and time and again you can have views of the islands in the lake.

A barn door, as it can still be found at old farmhouses

Irises

Red campion

Near Gstadt; Mount Hochfelln and Mount Hochgern in the background

Wild ducks are only temporary guests on Lake Chiemsee which in spring they pass on their way to their breeding areas in the north

Seebruck

The bridge across the River Alz gave the town at the northern-most point of the lake its name. The Romans who had erected a fort here, called the lake "Lucus Bedaius". One of several Roman roads traversing the Chiemgau connected Salzburg with Augsburg. Near Seebruck it was necessary to built a bridge across the River Alz. Travelling by car along the northern shore, you use the same route that the Romans determined at the beginning of our calendar. Apart from foundations of old Roman villas, a lot of fixtures, trinkets and tableware dating from that time have been uncovered in Seebruck.

Archaeological finds of all types can be viewed in the interesting Roman museum next to the church. If you follow the lakeside road in a western direction, you will pass a wooden building at the rim of the town. Inside is the well-preserved foundation of a Roman villa. Remarkably, the villa featured a floor heating system.

Klostersee (monastery lake) with the monastery of Seeon

Autumn in Seebruck

The marina in Seebruck

Left:
The marina in Seebruck

The two onion domes of
the monastery of Seeon

Brook near Seebruck

Right:
View of Lake Chiemsee
from Rimsting.
The mountains on the
horizon are called
Teisenberg, Hochstau-
fen, Zwiesel, Rausch-
berg, Hochfelln and
Hochgern

Spring in the "Schaf-
wascherbucht" (sheep
washing bay) with
Mount Kampenwand

*The colourful boats
in a sailing school*

Prien on Lake Chiemsee has been a market town since 1438. Nearby the River Prien runs into the lake

Right:
Winter on Lake Chiemsee

Double page (overleaf):
Sunset near Seebruck on Lake Chiemsee

Umratshausen with Mount Kampenwand

Chieming

Chieming on the eastern shore of Lake Chiemsee is the oldest settlement on the lake shore. In the large, curved bay you can find the most extensive pebble and sand beaches of Lake Chiemsee. Archaeological finds prove that the Roman road connecting Salzburg and Augsburg passed through the place. The knoll on which the parish church stands served the Roman occupying forces as a citadel. When in 1812 the old St Peter's Church was demolished, remains of Roman foundations were found. Some of these even bore inscriptions. Since neither the parson nor the forester could decipher them, they were not taken any further note of. In the bell house of the parish church three Roman altar stones, dedicated to the god of the lake, Bedaius, are kept.

Walking from the parish church with its flèche to the lake shore, you get to the water directly after an inn called "Unterwirt".
From here you have a fantastic view of Weitsee (broad lake), as the eastern part of the lake is called. There is hardly a spot on the eastern shore that offers a nicer vista of the Chiemgau mountains as well as some peaks in Tyrol.

Following the lake path in a northern direction, you will pass Schloss Chieming, formerly known

The parish church in Chieming

54

Lake shore near Chieming

as Neuenchieming. Until the 17th century, this castle was the seat of the "Hofmarksherr" (a kind of lord of the manor).

A former owner of the castle, the lawyer Dr Niklas Riebeisen from Augsburg, amassed a huge fortune when at the time of Reformation he proceeded against the Protestants and, by reason of his merits, was later employed by the Archbishop of Salzburg to quell the peasant uprising of 1525/26. After the leaders of the peasants were mercilessly killed, Riebeisen was rewarded with highly lucrative stakes in salt trade. Until 1965, the castle served as a parsonage. Today it is private property.

Schloss Chieming, an old castle

55

Right:
Schloss Hohenaschau

The Chiemgau Alps

The Chiemgau Alps include the pre-Alpine mountains between the River Saalach in the east and the River Inn in the west. The highest peak is Mount Sonntagshorn (1961 m). The Chiemgau Alps extend over 50 km (from east to west) and 23 km (from north to sourth). To the north the mountains are bordered by plains. Between Reichenhall and Rosenheim, the motorway connecting Munich and Salzburg can be regarded as the northern border of the Chiemgau Alps.

Since the lake once extended to the foot of the mountains, there is a large moor landscape between its present southern shore and the mountains. The best known of these mountains, which also account for the typical Chiemsee panorama, are Hochfelln, Hochgern, Hochplatte and Kampenwand. Hochfelln (1674 m) and Kampenwand (1668 m) can be reached by cable car. The valley station of Hochfelln cable car is in Bergen, the top station is only a few metres below the summit. This is not so on Mount Kampenwand: the top station lies at an altitude of 1460 metres, so if you want to stand on the summit, you will have to walk up the remaining 200 altimeters on a romantic footpath. The valley station of the cable car is in Hohenaschau in the Prien valley. Both peaks offer a magnificent view of the pre-Alps on one side and of the high mountains on the other.

In the valley of the River Tiroler Ache, which runs into Lake Chiemsee near Grabenstätt, some of the most famous tourist resorts in Bavaria are situated, among them Marquartstein, Unterwössen or Schleching. The latter two places are ideal starting points for an ascent of Mount Hochgern (1744 m). At a closer look, or else during an ascent, the wonderfully shaped mountain turns out to be a mountain range consisting of several peaks. With good reason it is considered one of the best panorama mountains in the Chiemgau. In good weather conditions you can make out the outlines of the Bavarian Forest in the north. In the south you discern the arc of the Bavarian and Tyrolese Alps – from the mountains around Berchtesgaden and the Loferer Steinberge all the way to the Kaiergebirge and many other ranges.

*Boats in the Schaf-
wascherbucht (sheep
wahing bay), with
Mount Kampenwand
in the background*

Evening on Mount Kampenwand. From up here one has a brilliant view of Lake Chiemsee

Winter on Mount Geigelstein;
in the background the Kaisergebirge range with its many peaks

Right: Marquartstein with Mount Hochplatte

View of Unterwössen and the valley of the River Tiroler Ache
from Mount Hochgern. On the horizon the mountain range of
Wilder Kaiser and the chain of the Central Alps

Steinplatte against Kaisergebirge

On Winklmoos-Alm

Reit im Winkl

You get to Reit im Winkl via Oberwössen and Moserpass (780 m). The southernmost parish of the Chiemgau is situated in a wide, sunny valley at the border to Tyrol. The region is exceptionally rich in snow, and every winter there are Nordic skiing competitions on an international level. The main reason for the abundance of snow is the fact that the valley is only open on its western side so that snow clouds are actually entrapped and detained. In and around Reit im Winkl, 400 kilometres of well-kept cross-country ski-tracks are prepared. Non-skiers can walk for several kilometres on footpaths which are cleared from snow for that reason.

In summer, too, the town – in typical upper-Bavarian style and officially recognized as a health resort – has a lot to offer: tennis, horse riding, a heated outdoor swimming pool, an 18-hole golf course, and numerous public footpaths.

At the time of the Congress of Vienna (1815), when after Napoleon's abdication the statesmen of Europe gathered and divided the continent, the place was so unknown and unimportant that it was almost forgotten. Legend has it that Prince-Elector Maximilian I of Bavaria, Emperor Franz of Austria and the Bishop of Salzburg played a card game to decide who would get the remote village of Reit in the back of beyond between the three countries. Maximilian was lucky and with the jack of diamonds decided the game in his favour. This anecdote is recorded in a painting on the wall of Gasthaus Unterwirt, an inn next to the parish church.

Mount Hörndlwand

Winter in Reit im Winkl

Right:
Reit im Winkl lies in
a gentle valley. In
the background the
mountain range of the
Kaisergebirge

Double page (overleaf):
Lake Weitsee with
Mount Gurrwand

Driving on the Deutsche Alpenstraße in the direction of Ruhpolding, you pass the car park of Seegatterl, from where in summer you can drive up the toll road to the famous Winklmoosalm (1183 m), a wonderful area for hikes. For example, you can walk up the highest of the surrounding mountains, Dürrbachhorn (1776 m). In winter the road is closed, but shuttle buses take skiers up to the lifts on Winklmoos – the home of Rosi Mittermeier, who, unforgettably, won two gold medals and one silver medal for Germany in the Olympic Games of 1976. With 13 ski lifts (19.500 people can be carried in one hour!) and 50 kilometres of groomed ski runs the skiing area of Winklmoosalm-Steinplatte (740-1870 m) leave nothing to be desired. In most years, up there the season starts as early as November.

The road from Seegatterl to Ruhpolding runs through the nature reserve of the Chiemgau Alps. It includes four lakes: Weitsee, Mittersee, Lödensee and Forchensee. This section of the Deutsche Alpenstraße ranks among the most beautiful of the whole route. By the way, on October 24, 1835, the last bear of the Chiemgau Alps was shot in this region (near Laubau).

In the area around Weitsee, Lödensee and Mittersee, the cross-country skier finds innumerable possibilities

*Mysterious
Lake Weitsee*

*Spring on Lake
Lödensee between
Ruhpolding and
Reit im Winkl*

Ruhpolding

Inzell and Ruhpolding, together with Reit im Winkl, form the so-called "Chiemgau holiday triangle". Ruhpolding was probably settled in the 9th and 10th centuries by the Baiuvarii, who came from the direction of Inzell. At that time the valley was called "Miesenbachertal" (from Middle High German "Mies" = swamp, moor). One possible reason for the settlement was that in this impassable forest valley the people wanted to take cover from the invading Hungarians.

They remained and cultivated the land. Until the end of the 19th century farming and forestry were the most important branches of the economy. The place was first mentioned in a document of 924 AD. After repeated changes of reign, the area came to Bavaria in 1275. A ducal office was established, and as early as 1424 a tavern is mentioned (the present "Hotel zur Post"). In 1467 the abbess of Frauenchiemsee had marble from Ruhpolding – much in demand even at that time – used for the construction of the convent church. The remote valley became better known when from 1529 onwards the Bavarian dukes realized that the Miesbach valley was rich in deer and regularly went there for hunting.

In 1619 the salt-works in Traunstein were opened. For centuries, woodcutting and log driving were indispensable sources of income for the farmers of Miesbach. The wood was needed to provide the brine-pans with firewood. In addition, mining flourished on Mount Rauschberg and Mount Unternberg in the 16th and 17th centuries. Lead ore and calamine were mined. The smelting-works at the foot of Mount Rauschberg, today called the "Schmelz" (between Ruhpolding and Inzell), dates from that time.

Ruhpolding in the valley of the River Weiße Traun with Mount Rauschberg on the left and Mount Sonntagshorn in the middle

Sport plays an important part in Ruhpolding. It is especially biathlon which time and again comes into the limelight of world public. Four world championships have already taken place here. The world cup competitions, regularly staged in January, are among the highlights of the season. Ruhpolding was one of the first villages in the Chiemgau to campaign for tourism. At first only a sideline and only hesitantly accepted by the locals, today tourism is the most important economic factor by far.

The churches in Ruhpolding, of which St George's Church is the largest and most beautiful, are well worth seeing. A cable car ride up Mount Rauschberg (1671 m) can be highly recommended.

The signpost shows some of many walking destinations

*The big water wheel
can be admired in the
Holzknechtmuseum
(woodcutter musuem)*

*Ruhpolding is one of the
most popular tourist destinations in the Chiemgau.
The mountains have just
the right height for wal-
king. The place with its
beautiful old houses is
very neat and cosy.
All kinds of recreational
facilities make for agree-
able holidays*

73

Inzell – Einsiedel

Left:
Village well and May pole in the centre of Ruhpolding

Works of art created by frost

75

Inzell

Inzell (700 m), a health resort and winter sport venue, lies in a wide valley rich in small waters. The surrounding mountains reach heights of up to about 1800 metres.

The parish has become somewhat famous because it is the site of the federal centre of high performance ice speed skating. In parallel with the development of the grounds, the number of overnight stays increased rapidly. The history of the origins of this centre is remarkable: Lake Frillensee (923 m), one of the coldest lakes in Germany, is part of Inzell's municipal area. Many years back, it was considered to use the 280-metre-long and 165-metre-wide lake for ice skating on a larger scale, but these plans came to naught due to frequent heavy snows in winter. In 1959, one more attempt to establish Lake Frillensee as an official centre of training and competition for ice speed skaters was ventured. When a commission of the German ice sports federation went to examine the lake on November 8, 1959, a lot of people were already out, skating under a bright blue sky on the smooth, 20-centimetre-thick ice. The consultations which took place during a light meal in the nearby inn of Adlgaß, resulted in the following: motion granted, but under the condition that the parish keep the way to the lake clear of snow and undertake to tend the ice. In the subsequent euphoria it was not clear to anybody what that meant. The area is rich in snow and walking to the lake takes about an hour! All the same, the "Frillensee venture" was on its way and was kept up for the next four years, in spite of all difficulties

As early as January 1960, the Bavarian and German ice speed skating championships were staged on Lake Frillensee to an audience of several thousand people. In the same year, the world record for long-distance curling was set up on the lake: 204,5 metres. In January 1962, 93 centimetres of snow fell in one night – of all nights, the night before the German championship! Thanks to the tireless efforts of a great number of voluntary helpers throughout the night, the competition could take place nevertheless. But the high frequency of adverse conditions eventually led to the abandonment of the "Frillensee project" and to the transfer of activities to natural ice on the grounds of the present centre of high performance.

In 1965 Germany's first ice rink featuring artificial ice was opened. The rink, which has been renovated several times, boasts state-of-the-art refrigeration technology and offers seats for 20.000 people. By now it has stood the test in nine world championship events, several European championships and dozens of national and international mass rallies. The 400-metre-long rink around a 30 m x 60 m surface of ice in the centre is divided into two competition rinks and one training rink, each 4 metres wide. As far as technology, functionality and comfort are concerned, the rink as well as the additional training and service facilities meet highest standards. Since 1966, 83 world records for ice speed skating alone have been set up here.

Inzell is reached via an impressive section of the Deutsche Alpenstraße, which runs through the gorge of the Weißbachschlucht. In the so-called "Gletschergarten" (glacier garden), a natural monument right after Zwing, you can see rocks cut smooth by the Saalach Glacier during the Würm Ice Age.

It is not far from here to the south-eastern-most corner of Bavaria and the magnificent high mountain landscape of the Berchtesgaden Alps. The Weißbachschlucht gorge is the bottleneck of the entry from the north-west.

Inzell with Mount Kienberg and Mount Rauschberg

Siegsdorf

77

Traunstein

To the east of Lake Chiemsee and to the north of the "Chiemgau holiday triangle" lies the major district town of Traunstein. As far as the origin of the name is concerned, legend has it that in former times a waggoner with a heavy load wanted to cross a ford of the River Traun. When the wagon was in the middle of the river and would neither move forth nor back, the man started to curse – at the same time that in nearby Haslach the bell was being rung to call people to prayer. "I wish everything turned into stone!" the waggoner shouted, and instantly horse, man and wagon turned into a big stone which can still be spotted near the river when approaching the town from the east. The prominent boulder has always stimulated the imagination of the people. In actual fact, the name of the River Traun in connection with "Stein", a word formerly used for a castle or a fortified place, neither goes back to a petrified waggoner nor to any other event, but to a castle or settlement on the River Traun.

It is true that in the listings of commodities belonging to the Church of Salzburg (with these listings dating from the year 790 AD), there are hints of possessions in the environs of Traunstein, but little is known about the early history of the settlement. It was first mentioned as "Trauwenstein" in 1245 AD. Until 1275, the Chiemgau and therefore also Traunstein belonged to the Archdiocese of Salzburg, but then the region fell to the share of the House of Wittelsbach that had reigned in Bavaria since 1180 AD.

Its location near the border to the Archdiocese of Salzburg, on a knell above the River Traun and at the place where the most important salt trade route from Reichenhall to Munich crossed the

Right:
The town of Traunstein with Mount Hochfelln and Mount Hochgern

The town square of Traunstein with Linden-brunnen (linden tree fountain) and Jaklturm, a rebuilt tower formerly called Salzburg gate

81

The facade of Marienapotheke, an old chemist's

Ludwigstraße, a street in the centre of Traunstein

river, made the settlement highly interesting for the new rulers.

It was enlarged and fortified. The importance of the town increased when in 1617 a brine pipeline was laid from Reichenhall to Traunstein. The saltworks of Traunstein was in operation until the year 1910.

Until the Middle Ages, salt, the "white gold", was the most important economic factor for the settlement. Traunstein was granted the town charter in 1375. It was largely spared the atrocities of the 30 Years' War, but not those of the plague which raged in 1635/36. In 1704 the Hungarian Pandurs set fire to the town, and in 1851 an even more devastating fire laid waste to almost the whole town. Due to the enormous industry of the citizens, it was reconstructed in only a few years in spite of a cholera epidemic.

About 18.000 people live in Traunstein today. The town offers 14.000 jobs, mainly in the fields of middle-class handicraft and trade, education, administration and services. It is a historically grown centre of the Chiemgau.

One of Traunstein's shopping streets is Bahnhofstraße, which leads directly into the town centre

Berchtesgadener Land

The Berchtesgadener Land comprises the area around the market town of Berchtesgaden, the territory formerly ruled by the prince provosts. It includes the well-known parishes of Ramsau, Schönau am Königssee, Bischofswiesen and Marktschellenberg. Besides, Berchtesgaden National Park with Mount Watzmann and Lake Königssee, Obersalzberg and the spa town of Bad Reichenhall lie within the borders of the administrative district of the Berchtesgadener Land. The proximity to Salzburg makes a visit to the city of Mozart almost obligatory.

Bad Reichenhall

It takes less than half an hour to drive from Berchtesgaden to Bad Reichenhall, the Bavarian state spa. It is situated in a wide, wind-protected basin-shaped valley, run through by the River Saalach and surrounded by several mountains, namely Staufen, Zwiesel, Müllnerhorn, Lattengebirge and Untersberg. In a north-eastern direction the basin opens towards the foothills. It can be reasoned from findings that the valley was already settled in the Stone Age (4000 years ago) and in the Bronze Age. The history of Reichenhall is the history of its salt (reich-an-hall = Celtic for: rich in salt). When the Romans got there after crossing the Alps, they came upon considerable facilities for boiling brine. These the Romans extended, and they also built salt roads along which trading with the then precious "white gold" was brisk. In the Middle Ages Reichenhall was ruled first by the Archbishops of Salzburg, later

Bad Reichenhall, a small town, but a great spa; surrounded by majestic mountains and run through by the River Saalach

by the Bavarian dukes. The history of the town is marked by devastating fires and floods.

In 1196 the Archbishop of Salzburg took punitive action and had Reichenhall burned down for the first time.

Other big fires were caused by carelessness, or else they sprang from the boiling pans at the saltworks, and each time almost the whole town burnt down. Disastrous high waters of the River Saalach repeatedly destroyed the log driving grounds beyond Luitpold Bridge ("Salzburg Weir"), from where the fire wood for the saltworks – which had been driven there from far away – was conducted via an elaborate canal system to the wood storage yards in the town. Today, nothing is left of these canals. As if there

had not been enough curses, the plague, too, claimed many victims in the 16th and 17th centuries.

After the last firestorm in 1834, the town was gradually established as a health resort. Reichenhall, which has been a spa since 1890 and a state spa since 1899, owes its present significance to the brine springs in the mountain range of the Lattengebirge. At the foot of Gruttenstein, in the so-called "Quellenbau", 22 natural brine springs issue from the ground. They have a salt content of up to 24%. The town's international reputation as a specialized spa for respiratory illnesses (particularly asthma and chronic bronchitis) as well as for rheumatic disorders is mainly due to these brine springs. Apart from brine, oils and extracts from mountain pine growing in the surrounding

The spa gardens in Bad Reichenhall

In Weißbach an der Alpenstraße, a May pole is being set up

Lake Thumsee between Inzell and Bad Reichenhall

Town hall

Spa gardens

mountains are applied. A large number of spa facilities and sanatoriums are available.

A number of sights in Reichenhall are well worth visiting: the old saltworks where, in the "Quellenbau" below the main well house, the brine springs bubble (guided tour and salt museum), the graduation works and the brine fountain in the spa gardens, the old part of the town around Florianiplatz (Floriani square), the Rathausplatz (townhall square) and the extensive pedestrian zone, the local museum and some churches, in particular St Zeno Minster and the parish church of St Nikolaus. In the "Kurgastzentrum", built in 1988, the spa guest finds the state spa administration as well as a gambling casino and a theatre hall.

A cable car ride up Mount Predigtstuhl can definitely be recommended. The cable car, one of Germany's first, was built as early as 1927/28. Since then, six million guests have been carried up to the top station (1583 m) in 8 $\frac{1}{2}$ minutes. The hotel added to the top station was built in the style of the 1930s. The view from up there is really impressive: deep down you can see the Reichenhall basin, which towards the foothills is bordered by Mount Hochstaufen and Mount Zwiesel; to the south the massive ranges of the Bechtesgaden Alps hulk up. Around Reichenhall, 150 kilometres of well-marked walking paths have been prepared. Lake Thumsee is one of the most beautiful natural bathing lakes far and wide. A visit to a small pond covered by water lilies at the eastern end of the lake ("Seemösl") can be highly recommended.

Right:
Reichenhaller Haus, a
mountain hut near the top
of Mount Hochstaufen.
View of Piding, the motor-
way and Salzburg

Berchtesgaden

The market town of Berchtesgaden lies at an altitude of 540-600 metres in the unique setting of the Berchtesgaden Alps including Mount Watzmann. In the 900-year-long history of the Berchtesgadener Land the locality has kept its standing as a traditional hub and largely preserved its beautiful overall appearance. The car-free centre features neat old houses, streets and squares as well as ample town houses and magnificent churches. Berchtesgaden lies on the River Ache and has 7800 inhabitants. With its still profitable salt mine, it is not only a tourist magnet, but also a health resort.

The nearby valleys of the River Saalach and the River Salzach had already been settled for a long time when, at the beginning of the 12th century, four Augustine monks from the monastery of Rottenbuch in Ammergau set forth by order of Count Berengar of Sulzbach (near Amberg) to found a monastery in the undeveloped mountain valley. Eventually, after considerable difficulties, a monastery and a church were erected. The church was consecrated in 1122. This was the primordial cell of Berchtesgaden. The monks called settlers into the area to cultivate the land. They were given land as "Lehen" (from geliehen = lent). In return they had to hand over a substantial part of their yield. After its foundation it took less than two centuries until the tiny monastic state had developed into an autonomous Papal State ("Fürstpropstei Berchtesgaden" = territory of the prince provosts of Berchtesgaden). The territorial lord, the provost, held all conceivable capacity which otherwise only the emperor possessed: forest, hunting and mining rights as well as unlimited high justice.

In contrast to the capitularies, who mostly were of noble descent and who soon gave up their Spartan life at the monastery, the rural population starved for centuries. At first, sparse yields from arable farming and cattle breeding formed the basis of existence, until salt mining opened up additional sources of income. Finally, from the 15th century onwards, large parts of the population scraped along on the money earned by the manufacture of the so-called "Berchtesgadener War" (goods from Berchtesgaden) – home-made products like wooden toys, crib figurines, painted chipboard boxes and the like, which were sold throughout Europe. The 700-year-long history of the monastic state is characterized by the permanent wrangling of its big neighbours Salzburg and Bavaria for salt from Berchtesgaden, but also by the continuing poverty and isolation of its inhabitants.

Right:
View of Berchtesgaden from Lercheck, with Mount Watzmann and Mount Hochkalter in the background

Berchtesgaden with Mount Untersberg in winter

Spa gardens in Berchtesgaden and Mount Watzmann

In 1803, the collapse of the "Holy Roman Empire of the German Nation" signified the end of Berchtesgaden's autonomy. During the following seven years, the sovereign changed four times, until in 1810 Berchtesgaden finally became part of Bavaria. At the beginning of the 19th century Berchtesgaden experienced a greater change than ever before in its century-long history. In 1803 the dissolution of the monastic state in the course of Secularisation brought about the preconditions for a development that was overdue in the until then almost completely isolated land: it was opened up. Scientists, some of them also climbers, as well as painters and writers were the first to visit the almost unknown basin at the foot of Mount Watzmann. In a little while, their reports and pictures of a wonderful landscape made Berchtesgaden widely known.

Soon the number of guests increased considerably, and more and more locals found employment in tourism.

A dark chapter of the German past is connected with Obersalzberg, which lies to the north-east of Berchtesgaden. When Adolf Hitler recognized the charm of the former health resort, he initiated the establishment of a centre of power and control of the Third Reich from 1933 onwards. It was destroyed by the bombs of the allies on April 25, 1945.

After the war the number of guests in Berchtesgaden rose again. Today most of the inhabitants live directly or indirectly of tourism.

The scenic sights of the area have often been effusively praised. "Festival of nature" is the new slogan of tourist advertising in Berchtesgaden. It is hardly possible to find a better one! It seems as if in this south-eastern-most corner of Bavaria nature had dug deep into her cornucopia one more time: massive mountain ranges with jagged ridges beside more moderate plateau mountains; steep rock faces beside grass-covered mountain flanks; the highest rock face of the Eastern Alps (east face of Mount Watzmann); the northernmost glacier of the Alps (Blaueis on Mount Hoch-

kalter); charming valleys, green like the valley of Maria Gern or filled with debris like the Wimbach Valley, which is embedded between mighty rock walls; all kinds of waters, for example cheerful streams, fjord-like Lake Königssee, dark Lake Obersee, romantic Lake Hintersee, as well as some ice-cold mountain lakes lying at altitudes of more than 1500 metres; Germany's biggest glacial cave, that of Schellenberg on Mount Untersberg.

The Mount Jenner cable car (1874 m) makes it possible for you to view the massive rock plateau of the mountain ranges of Hagengebirge and Steinernes Meer without your having to exert yourself. You can ride on a mine train into the salt

Small hay barn near a farmhouse called Marxenlehen; view of Berchtesgaden and Mount Watzmann

93

Berchtesgaden: Stiftkirche (convent church) and Schlossbrunnen (castle fountain)

mine underneath the Haselgebirge, or you can drive the circular Rossfeld mountain road, which offers fantastic panoramic views of the Berchtesgaden basin and of the Salzkammergut area in Austria. Buses take visitors up to Mount Kehlstein, the site of Hitler´s former Tea Room, which today is a cosy mountain restaurant. Last but not least, there are a number of historical churches and museums waiting for those interested.

Apart from Berchtesgaden, four other parishes lie in the basin at the foot of Mount Watzmann: Schönau am Königssee, Ramsau, Bischofswiesen and Marktschellenberg.

Ramsau near Berchtesgaden with the mountain range of Reiteralpe

Berchtesgaden Alps

Berchtesgaden Alps is the name of a part of the Northern Limestone Alps including not only the mountains of the Berchtesgadener Land, but also some mountains in the Salzburger Land lying on the Austrian side of the border. The nine mountain ranges which belong to the Berchtesgaden Alps are bordered by the River Saalach in the west and the River Salzach in the east. In the north they almost reach Salzburg. The southern border is defined by a line connecting Saalfelden (near Lake Zeller See), Dienten and Mühlbach on Mount Hochkönig. The main massifs are: Watzmann in the centre, annularly surrounded by Lattengebirge, Untersberg, Hoher Göll, Hagengebirge with Steinernes Meer, Hochkönig, Hochkalter and Reiteralpe (also called Reiteralm). The height of the mountains decreases from south to north. The highest point is Mount Hochkönig (2941 m), which lies on Austrian territory and is covered by a plateau glacier (Übergossene Alm). The mountain range of Lattengebirge near Bad Reichenhall only reaches a height of 1700 metres. The highest peak on German territory is the so-called "Mittelspitze" (middle peak) of Mount Watzmann with a height of 2713 metres.

Most of the mountain area is part of a national park which was founded in 1978 by the Bavarian State Government. The "Alpenpark Berchtesgaden" (forefield of the national park) is nearly identical with the territory of the former monastic state of Berchtesgaden (Fürstpropstei, i.e. territory of the prince provosts). It comprises 46.000 hectares, indeed a respectable size by Middle European standards. The national park proper evolved from the former Königssee Nature Reserve and comprises 21.000 hectares. The inner zone

consists of Reiteralpe, Hochkalter, Watzmann, Hoher Göll, Hagengebirge and Steinernes Meer, including the valleys of Klausbach and Wimbach, two mountain streams, and that of Lake Königssee. Here nature preservation has absolute priority. Nature is left to itself, without any human interference. All animals and plants are protected.

Mount Watzmann

Without any doubt, the most famous mountain of the Berchtesgaden Alps is Watzmann.
"Once upon a time there ruled in Berchtesgaden a king who ruthlessly oppressed his people.

On Mount Untersberg: Berchtesgadener Hochthron on the right and Mount Watzmann and the mountain range of Steinernes Meer on the horizon

Left:
Mount Watzmann seen from Steinernes Meer

97

He despised the good, was only fond of hunting, and his subjects trembled when they heard the noise of the bugles, the barking of the dogs and the pounding of the horses. By day and by night the mad hunting party rushed through forests and chasms, persecuted the deer and destroyed the seed. One day the king appeared on a clearing where a herd of cattle were grazing. The herdswoman was sitting in front of a hut, her sleeping child in her arm. The herding dog was lying beside her. Suddenly the king's hounds darted upon the herding dog and caused the terrified woman to fall to the ground. When the herdsman came running and struck blows at the howling pack, the king, inflamed with rage, set his churls and dogs on the herdsman, and he as well as his wife and child were mauled. At that moment there was a grumbling noise and a terrible thunderstorm started. Since then the king and his family, turned into cold stone, have been standing high above the land which formerly they ruled so cruelly."

This is how the well-known legend explains the formation of the highest mountain around Berchtesgaden.

Seen from the market town it presents its most striking shape, with its peaks of varying height:

on the right, Hocheck (2653 m), the first summit of the Watzmann ridge, which runs in a south-western direction to Mittelspitze (middle peak, 2713 m) and Südspitze (south peak, 2712 m); and on the left, Kleiner Watzmann (little Watzmann, also called "Watzmannfrau", Watzmann's wife; 2307 m). The wide cirque between the two peaks is called Watzmannkar. In the cirque five rocky spikes are noticeable, the Watzmannkinder (Watzmann's children), as they are called. On its right-hand side, the narrow main ridge drops steeply into the Wimbach Valley, on its left to the Watzmannkar, but beyond the Mittelspitze the ridge drops to the notorious Watzmann East Face. The characteristic form of Watzmann is best seen from Berchtesgaden. The Watzmann range offers an abundance of possibilities for mountain tours, from hiking to extreme rock climbing. There are three mountain huts which serve as bases, the most important of which is Watzmannhaus (1928 m) on the north-eastern side of Hocheck, established by the Munich section of the Alpine Club. Then there is Kührointhütte (1420 m) to the north-east of Kleiner Watzmann, a popular destination for day hikes. At the foot of Südspitze, on the south side of the mountain, is Wimbachgrieß-hütte (1327 m). An ascent of Watzmann-Hocheck does not pose a big problem for sure-footed mountaineers, if they spend the night at Watzmannhaus and do the climb in two days (total walking time about 6-7 hours). The traverse of the ridge to Südspitze should only be undertaken by experienced climbers!

A wonderful view of Mount Watzmann on the one side and the Berchtesgaden basin on the other can be obtained from Mount Grünstein (1304 m), a perfect vantage point.

In the Berchtesgadener Land, edelweiss can still be seen quite frequently, whereas in other areas this mountain flower has become rare

Lake Königssee

Lake Königssee is one of the chief attractions of the Berchtesgadener Land or even Bavaria.

The lake is some eight kilometres long and only 1 ½ kilometres wide and, embedded between the steep walls of Mount Watzmann and those of the mountain ranges of Hagengebirge and Steinernes Meer, resembles a fjord. It reaches a maximum depth of 189 metres. Since it is so deep and for the most part fed by subterranean springs, the water is rather cold even in summer. The lake owes its existence to the glaciers of the Ice Age which deepened the basin that had already been there before. When the ice retreated, the melting water accumulated in the valley. 10.000 years ago, the retreat of the glacier came to a temporary standstill in the area of the present Saletalm. The debris of the moraines formed a dam which was further enlarged by rockslides. When later the ice melted completely it was in the basin behind this wall of debris that Lake Obersee emerged.

The fine-sounding name of Königssee (king's lake) goes back to Chuno of Horburg, who reigned at the time of the foundation of the monastic state of Berchtesgaden. The lake was called "Chuni-See" after him. The name was later modified into "Kunosee" or "Kunigessee" and finally became "Königssee". Until 1909 green-white rowing boats were the only means of transport on the lake. Today visitors are carried by electric boats, which are specially constructed for Lake Königssee. The boats do not cause any pollution so that the lake's water still has the quality of drinking water. The boat trip is a fantastic experience.

In former times, the sevenfold echo was elicited by a gun-salute or pistol shot. Today a member of the crew plays a melody on the flugelhorn. The

Right:
Lake Königssee with St Bartholomä and the east face of Watzmann

sounds are echoed one or two times by the steep rock faces. Then the boat approaches the church of St Bartholomä with its shingle-covered red onion domes, doubtlessly one of the most famous sights of the Berchtesgadener Land. As early as 1134 a little chapel – according to an old document called "Basilica Chunigessee" – stood on this promontory. Apart from the convent church, this is the oldest church in the Berchtesgadener Land. In the background towers the almost 2000 metre-high Watzmann East Face, an allure for every climber. Since its first ascent on June 6, 1881, more than 100 people have lost their lives on this rock wall.

Near the church and the hunting lodge, which has served as a restaurant since 1919, there are only three more buildings: the boat house at the lake shore, a fisherman's house and a forester's lodge. Even though the promontory of St Barholomä ranks among the most visited tourist attractions,

it has preserved much of its primordial state. There is no hotel or other overnight accommodation at Bartholomä. Even most of the employees leave at the end of the day and take the boat to go home. There is no land access apart from some mountain paths, and it takes several hours to walk on those to Bartholomä. The shores of the lake are too steep for an easy land access.

From Salet, the end of the line of the Königssee boats, it takes about 10 minutes to get to the much smaller Lake Obersee. It is 1200 metres long and 500 metres wide and lies 11 metres higher than Königssee. A small stream connects the two lakes.

Hoher Göll and Hohes
Brett are reflected in
Lake Hintersee